HOW TO PLAY BASEBALL

FOR KIDS

Special Edition

2019 By Tony R. Smith. All Rights Reserved

TABLE OF CONTENTS

INTRODUCTION 4

CHAPTER ONE...7

    WHAT ARE BASEBALL TRADING PINS? 7

    BASEBALL RULES - A MUST FOR BEGINNERS............................11

INSTRUCTING BASEBALL RULES AND SKILLS TO YOUR CHILD 15

BASEBALL - RULES AND HISTORY 18

BASEBALL EQUIPMENT BAGS ARE A MUST FOR THE SERIOUS
TRAVEL PLAYER 22

CHAPTER TWO.. 26

EXCITING POINTS WHEN BUYING YOUR BASEBALL EQUIPMENT
BAG.. 26

    STRATEGIES FOR THE CATCHER IN BASEBALL 33

SPEEDING THE GAME OF BASEBALL UP 37

SEVEN STEPS ON HOW TO HIT A BASEBALL 41

THE MOST EFFECTIVE METHOD TO ANALYZE A BASEBALL SWING
.... 44

CHAPTER THREE.. 50

HOW TO PITCH A BASEBALL: A DETAILED DESCRIPTION OF THE
SEQUENCE OF MOVES.. 50

DISTINCTIVE TYPES OF PITCHES IN BASEBALL 53

BASEBALL DRILLS - INFIELD CRISPNESS IS KEY............................56

BASEBALL COACHING DIGEST - BASEBALL RULES - UNDERSTANDING THE "INFIELD FLY" RULE 59

A PEEK ON THE MAJOR LEAGUE BASEBALL RECORDS............,,,,,,,......64

COACHING YOUTH BASEBALL - TIPS TO BE SUCCESSFUL WITHOUT ALIENATING PARENTS 70

12 STEPS FOR PARTNTS AND COACH RELATIONSHIP.......................75

CONCLUSION 86

DISCLOSURE STATEMENT...90

WORKOUT NOTES..91

INTRODUCTION

What do baseball players and mentors think about amid the offseason? In ongoing talks, I discovered that one unique theme of the discussion was baseball preparing. Mentors need to urge their players to take an interest in baseball preparing, and numerous players need to utilize that opportunity to get ready for one year from now.

Numerous players choose to utilize the offseason to enhance their playing aptitudes. They need to play better when the following spring season arrives. To do this, a lot of children play fall ball, or they take part in winter baseball camps. They need however much preparing as could reasonably be expected, not exclusively to improve their aptitudes yet additionally, so they don't lose the abilities they as of now have.

It's a smart thought that all secondary school players consider all year baseball preparing. Indeed, even the more youthful players (ages 12-14) would profit by needing to take their abilities to the following dimension.

With the correct preparation, they would be progressively arranged for secondary school baseball.

In case you're worried about the chilly climate, there are indoor offices accessible everywhere throughout the nation. Furthermore, a lot of schools enables understudy competitors to rehearse in the rec center on specific occasions. I've even observed advertisements that idea as long as multi-day facilities amid the offseason at reasonable costs.

In case you're amidst a season, exploit this time by improving yourself and increasing practical experience. Discover some time among diversions and practice to get in as much baseball preparing as you can. This will help you in the late spring and fall seasons.

You ought to likewise think about a baseball-specific exercise, molding and a regular sustenance program. These will provide all the assistance you. If you eat ineffectively amid the off-season, you'll have the capacity to tell in the spring. You should be lean and reliable to play well, so make sure to eat a lot of organic products, vegetables, nuts, seeds and healthy fats like avocados.

You can likewise profit by baseball preparing by perusing and watching baseball materials. Baseball is about half mental, so it doesn't merely require physical practice. Investigate purchasing great baseball hitting books and study them cautiously. You'll discover a lot of incredible tips to help you in your circumstance. Additionally, watch proficient amusements slowly to perceive how the stars play.

Baseball preparing is significant for all secondary school players and something they should consider if they are not kidding about the game. The offseason shouldn't merely be an opportunity to unwind and eat vast amounts of awful sustenance. Baseball ought to be thought of as an all year energy.

CHAPTER ONE

What Are Baseball Trading Pins?

The pins are of extraordinary significance in the sport of baseball. These are utilized as enhancing things on the garments of players of baseball crews. Every game has its cards. Every group arranges these cards at the beginning of the period.

All groups purchase these pins for whole season ahead of time and in a tremendous amount. Baseball has its one of a kind spot in America because of that it replaces national game there. Because of this, it has a colossal after there. These pins come in various sizes, styles, designs and so forth.

These things appear amid the time of the 1980s when Olympic was held at New York. However, authoritatively the exchanging pins utilized in baseball sports in 1983, from that point forward pretty much every tournament has a function where the groups traded there pins with one another. Already identifications are utilized to make the player distinguished for which country or group they are speaking to. These pins not just develop the assurance of the player yet, also, a decent cash making source. They can be gotten as in various varieties, for example, group, players and mentor pins and so forth.

Children and grown-ups both are aficionados of gathering these exchanging pins. Children don't care for collecting baseball pins, yet they like the preferred nails that have cartoon characters on them. They wear on their garments and show them to their companion. Devotees of baseball match-up have a one of a kind side interest of gathering exchanging pins of their preferred group or players. Rather than purchasing these pins, these days' individuals trade those pins with one another, so both get fulfilled.

Fans wear same sticks on their garments when they are cheering their groups to demonstrate to them that they are a piece of their group. They are utilized to enrich garments fundamentally. These are of low cost, yet some exceptional, antique pins are of enormous loss. For purchasing those, you need to try and burn through a large number of dollars. Gathering them in America is of extraordinary interest. For collecting pins, some unique sacks are accessible for this reason to convey pins with you for exchanging idea amid the tournaments.

Exchanging pins are well known and are a piece of every game nowadays whether it is tennis, cricket, swimming, hockey, soccer, softball, ball, yard tennis, and different sports too. The uniform is inadequate without the pins on it. It comes in various sizes; every group orders distinctive format and examples of their nails for the season.

Fundamentally the size differs between 1.50" to 3". The best size is 1.75" or 2". A lot greater pins are tiny in requests.

It comes in various styles, for example, danglers, blinkers, bobbleheads, glittery, made of pearl stones, sliders, spinners and so on they are implied like this to get the fascination of the watchers. Baseball neckline pins are made of sparkles with the goal that it imagines the player's name or the group name for which they are playing.

Baseball Rules - A Must For Beginners

Numerous young individuals watch baseball and become energetic to turn into a piece of a sorted out gathering of players. Usually, young players, unfamiliar with the principles of the amusement, choose to join a trainer to begin playing the diversion. Regularly, even the trainer overlooks the need to teach the players on the guidelines of the distraction.

Here are the essential standards for amateurs that they ought to realize when the season endures:

Keep it necessary for the youngsters and show the baseball rules with the batting request of the group, at the burrow. The umpire can announce a player out if the hitter did not pursue the batting request. While batting or running the base, a player needs to keep his cap on. For his first offense, the umpire issues a notice to the player and can announce him out, when he submits a second offense.

The strike zone is just about the width of the home plate (or somewhat more extensive), with tallness considered from the dimension of the knees, up to the shoulders of the hitter. The player needs to watch the strike zone. On hitting the baseball, it is necessary for the player to sprint to achieve a respectable starting point. If the pitched ball arrives inside the strike zone, however, the player abstains from swinging, the umpire will call a "strike."

A Batter gets three strikes, and Is Out Under The Following Conditions:

1) A defender gets the ball before it contacts the ground.

2)A defender tosses the ball to the first baseman, who contacts the base with his foot since the ball is in his grasp or glove.

3)A player of the handling group labels the hitter straightforwardly with the ball, or with the glove holding the ball before he securely achieves a respectable starting point.

4)Any player from the handling group labels the hitter straightforwardly with the ball or the glove holding the ball when the hitter is in transit to a respectable halfway point, third base, or home.

There are numerous guidelines for running starting with one base then onto the next. A sprinter is required to contact each station while approaching the infield and can score a run just on reaching the primary, second and third base, and afterward achieving the home plate, in that succession. While adjusting the bottom, a base sprinter isn't permitted to sidestep a kindred sprinter in his front. Further, he can't keep running past three feet from his pattern if he needs to avoid being labeled out, aside from while staying away from impedance with some defender. The sprinters need to work on sliding according to rules, in a sheltered and appropriate way.

For announcing a sprinter tag out, the defender needs to reach the sprinter, straightforwardly with the ball, or his glove, while he is holding the ball in a similar hand. When the defender contacts the sprinter with his glove, with the ball held in the other hand, it isn't out. The pitcher needs to try to have his one foot on the elastic, and should quickly go to a complete stop amid his windup. Further, a pitcher, while in the pitching circle, can't put any of his hands on his mouth, without the earlier endorsement of the umpire.

All players must realize the baseball principles to flawlessness. Association players are not permitted to contend strikes or balls, with the umpire. The players must regard the umpire's choice and esteem trainer's assessments. The referees reserve the option to exclude a player or mentor on having valid justifications.

Instructing Baseball Rules and Skills to Your Child

Ball games are games that you would love to watch. How the amusement is played gives you unexplained energy and rush. The object of baseball is to score a more significant number of keeps running than the restriction, and the technique lies in the constant battle between the offense and the resistance. If you need to show your kid how to play baseball and appreciate quality time with him through games, then you can do it with the assistance of the data on the essential abilities of this diversion.

Fundamentally, in tossing, the ball is typically grasped with the thumb on one side and the record and center fingers on the contrary hand. The weight of the fingers on the ball must generally be equivalent to the measure of the power of the toss. There are three kinds of toss, overhead toss, side toss, and underarm toss. They differ depending on the separation of the individual tossing the ball and the individual who will get it. In addition to the fact that distance is significant in utilizing tazer immobilizer, it is essential in this sort of diversion.

To get a low toss, you should show your tyke to reach with the glove on the ground inverse his body. If your child, for example, needs to be an outfielder, you should impart in his psyche to figure out how to pass judgment on the trip of the ball and get under it quick. The ball must be kept in front consistently. At the point when an outfielder is running back to get a long fly, his head ought to be turned on more than one occasion to recognize the ball and the fingers are pointed upwards. As a catcher, you should have a decent perspective on your objective which is the flying ball just like when you need an eye of your attacker when you have to release the tests of your taser firearm.

Additionally, pitching includes the windup, the delivery, and the finish to guarantee control. The motivation behind the windup is to create a smooth and natural distribution of the pitch. After delivery, as a pitcher, he should confront the plate decisively to be in a high position to handle any ball hit. You should show your tyke likewise about the strike zone which is straightforwardly over the plate, between the hitter's armpits and his knees.

Finally, you should show your child how to hit the ball. A decent batting necessitates that the whole body is balanced without hardly lifting a finger and impact. You can be the pitcher and give your child a chance to hold the baseball gear which is the bat. While hanging tight for the pitch, you should train your kid to put his body weight on the chunks of the feet, with hips, shoulders and eyes level and bat high. Upon the pitch, let your child whip the ball with free arm activity and snap of wrists and the two hands immovably holding the bat the full swing.

The fruitful procedure of learning and building up the aptitudes associated with baseball will rely upon consistent interest and legitimate disposition. You can build up the enthusiasm of your tyke in this sort of play by appropriate inspiration and gradually showing him the essential aptitudes and baseball rules.

Baseball - Rules and History

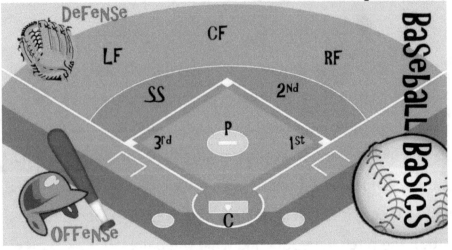

Baseball is a diversion played with a bat and ball. It is between two teams, every one of which has nine players. The winner of the game is the team that has scored more keeps running toward the finish of nine innings. Runs are scored by hitting a thrown ball with the bat and after that rushing to contact whatever number bases as would be prudent before the ball can be gotten and thrown back. The stations are organized in a 90-foot square called a baseball jewel.

The batting team alternates confronting the pitcher of the restricting team who remains amidst the precious stone on the pitcher's hill. The pitcher is upheld by the other eight players on his team who are exhibited to recover the ball rapidly after it is hit. They will likely prevent players from jumping on base (or progressing once they have arrived).

The objective of the hitter is to propel right around the jewel and in the extended run return to home plate, scoring a run. He can do this all alone (by hitting a grand slam) or by scoring on ensuring players' hits. One side successes when they have scored a higher number of keeps running than the other toward the finish of nine innings.

One turn at bat for each team establishes an inning; nine innings make up a baseball game. The teams switch among batting and handling at whatever point the handling team gets three outs on the batting team.

Baseball is identified with more than a couple of different games that include bats and balls. An early type of baseball, called rounders, was being played in England more than 250 years back. As the English and Irish workers came to America, they carried the game with them.

By the late 1800s, the game of baseball as we probably are aware it, had turned into the national distraction.

Baseball has likewise turned into a world game, being played novices and experts alike in North America, portions of Central and South America and the Caribbean, and parts of East and Southeast Asia. The game is here and there alluded to as hardball when contrasted with the set of softball which utilizes a bigger ball and is played by teams with more players.

In North America, proficient Major League Baseball is played by teams that are isolated into the National League (NL) and the American League (AL).

Each class has three divisions: East, West, and Central. Consistently, the victor of Major League Baseball is controlled by playoffs that peak in the World Series.

Each class produces four teams that make the playoffs. These teams are comprised of the three standard season division winners, in addition to one side (the "special case team") that has the best record of the nation-Division pioneers.

Each association plays by a somewhat unusual arrangement of standards. In the National League, the pitcher required to bat, per the standard guidelines. In the

American League, there is a tenth player, an assigned hitter, who hits for the pitcher, and who does not take the field when the restricting team strikes.

Each significant alliance team has a "ranch framework" of small-time organizations at different dimensions. These teams enable more youthful players to create as they gain on-field involvement against adversaries with approximate dimensions of aptitude.

Baseball Equipment Bags Are a Must For the Serious Travel Player

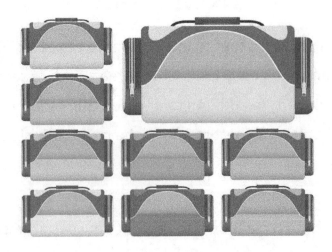

What precisely are Baseball Equipment Bags? These bags are a significant piece of baseball players' apparatus. They are offered in an array of models, textures, and hues. Each athletic baseball player ought to have baseball bags. They will make bats progressively convenient to transport starting with one diversion then onto the next. One can discover assortments of baseball bags - fundamental, utilitarian baseball bags, club baseball bags, baseball rucksack, batting bearers, roller baseball bags, duffle-style bags, getting gear bags etcetera. You can buy most gear bags at your squad at modest cost focuses.

The kinds of apparatus you are going to choose is probably going to rely on one's solicitations. Most, ballplayers are choosing lightweight bags which are connected similarly to baseball bat bags. Others are made to convey baseball spikes and other baseball gear. A lot of Fastpitch softball and baseball player bags are for players have fence cuts, additional pockets to have the capacity to hold your cash, I-Pods, remote telephones, and so forth. Besides, fastpitch softball and baseball bats have a ventilated footwear burrow segment, central stockpiling zone, incidental top concealed capacity territory, additionally downy areas for essential belongings. They've versatile cushioned neck and shoulder band alongside neoprene shutting conveying handles. Regardless of whether you get duffle-style baseball gear sack, you can discover enough space to carry the bats and have territories for hardware and baseballs.

Attempt a rucksack style bags if you need two hands allowed to transport more things. Most bearers incorporate shoulder ties just like a standard knapsack, and additionally, they highlight spaces for your bats to experience. They might be increasingly expensive. Moving baseball bags will, in general, be about things type transporters. Most have compartments for bats, baseballs and gloves combined with little wheels if you need to pull the sack and spring up handles to move it in and around. There are even vast models of such bags. Their value goes on measurement in addition to the dimension of value.

Remember that you will need to think about the materials of baseball hardware bags. Anyway, your decision needs to satisfy your very own needs and spending plan. Besides, the baseball bags produced using nylon can be more unstable when contrasted and those delivered from heavier canvas type materials, which creates a more grounded pack.

Group baseball bags can make your group look progressively gifted. Coordinating garments help baseball contenders to distinguish themselves with the group; these individuals seem increasingly like a gathering and in this way adopt the thought process of a group. Each baseball hardware sack may effortlessly be custom-made with your group's hues and altered logo. Squads with same tones and plans look great at competitions or youth baseball match-ups. It will give you just as your team a decent feeling of pride. "To be a group, you should initially look and feel, similar to a group." an old mentor of mine once said. Obtaining the proper baseball pack isn't a simple occupation. Remember that incredible baseball hardware bags can at present be bought effortlessly. You don't have to spend a ton of mixture on baseball hardware bags, locate a decent arrangement.

CHAPTER TWO

Exciting points When Buying Your Baseball Equipment Bag

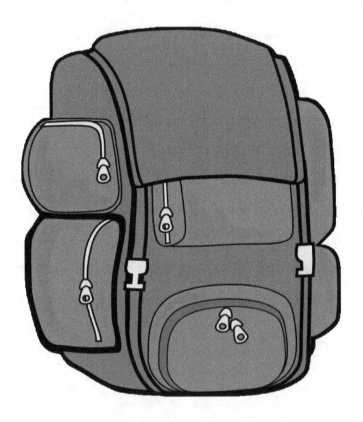

Wearing hardware required for baseball has developed with time. Bats, gloves, gloves, security gear like batting head protectors, chest defenders, visors and shin protectors, and baseball spikes have all moved toward becoming a piece of the existing standard hardware.

Hauling around this apparatus from amusement to practice can without much of a stretch become tedious particularly if you are utilizing an old duffel pack for capacity.

What's more, how about we not overlook that this hardware doesn't come modest. Also, with the measure of apparatus around, it's straightforward to miss an essential bit of equipment. There are not many more awful sentiments on a baseball field than strolling into the burrow, opening up your pack and understanding that you've overlooked your glove.

Because of current innovation, the present baseball bat bags are planned not exclusively to shield your rigging from mileage yet additionally to make them simple to bear. You don't have to endure a sore shoulder conveying round that old duffel sack! Baseball bat bags are additionally outfitted with exceptional pockets and pockets for various hardware including your iPods, mobiles, and wallets; being efficient turns into a breeze! You'll presently think that its difficult to overlook that glove!

The incredible assortment of baseball hardware bags around can without much of a stretch befuddle you. This little guide gives you the nuts and bolts to remember while making your baseball gear sack buy.

- First, assess the measure of gear you have to convey. There's no point purchasing a sack that is too huge or unreasonably little for your necessities!

- Make beyond any doubt your sack is made of the right materials. Nylon bags might be less expensive; however thicker canvas bags persevere through additional.

- The ideal sack is commonly two-layered; a final external layer to avoid harm and a padded internal layer to shield your gear from the mileage.

Baseball bat bags come in various styles. We should look at the major ones:

Standard Baseball Bat Bags:

These duffle-styled bags have been a staple of the diversion for quite a long time.

Search for:

- Durable polyester development

- Strong pulling handles for simple transportation

- Large stockpiling limit

- Multiple compartments for simple association and

- Fence snares to drape the bags on the whole fence effortlessly

Extraordinary: For increasingly prepared players and the individuals who need to bear a genuinely complete combination of apparatus

Knapsacks:

Attempt these when you need two hands-frees.

Search for:

- Padded back and bears for agreeable wear
- Durable development
- Bat sleeves to hold your bats
- Medium estimated primary compartment for your fundamental rigging
- Fence snares to balance the pack in the burrow
- Accessory pockets

Incredible: For brisk excursions to and from the jewel. Or on the other hand, if you merely need to pack a few nuts and bolts (glove, spikes and several bats)

Moving Baseball Bags:

They could be your standard baseball bat bags fitted with wheels, or they could be almost things type transporters.

Search for:

- Robust polyester development with fortified base for included sturdiness around the wheels
- Extendable take handles or Pop-up handles for effectively pulling them around

- Massive capacity limit

- Multiple compartments for simple association
- Fence snares

Extraordinary: For prepared players who need to bear a lot of hardware effortlessly

Group Equipment Bags:

Intended to hold a whole group of rigging.

Search for:

- Durable development

- Dugout compartments to keep gear protected and sorted out for simple access

Incredible: For Coaches, Equipment Manager and voyaging groups

Locate the best regarded online goal for baseball gear shopping including a broad scope of value, sturdy baseball hardware bags and baseball bat bags from the best producers. Whatever your requirements, you don't have far to look if you realize where to purchase!

Strategies For the Catcher in Baseball

I like others on the protection; the catcher in baseball has a task when the ball is hit. More often than not, it's guarding the plate. On pop-ups and hits, The play for the put-out is all the time all his. Regardless of what the match, the catcher should hurl his cover aside as fast as could reasonably be expected.

To handle the hit, the catcher (apparently right-gave) ought to dependably endeavor to go to the left of the ball- make a little circle if he can so he'll be in a high position to toss when he concocts it. When the ball is as yet rolling when the catcher achieves it, he should cut his glove down before it to stop the move, at that point scoop his glove and exposed hand together for the pickup. When the ball has ended, the catcher can make the pickup with the exposed side.

Catch It With Your Nose

On all pop-ups, the catcher needs to take care of business under the ball as fast as he can and be holding up as the ball descends. Since pop-ups to the catcher are brought about by a sharp undercut of the ball, the ball turns at an astounding rate. The turn will make the ball "move" toward some path however as a rule toward the infield.
The catcher must be cautious about this float as the ball

descends and not attempt to get it with the arms expanded, else he will all of a sudden find that his arms are two inches short!

To shield the ball from coasting distant, the catcher should keep his nose directly underneath it. "Catch it with your nose" the geniuses state. (It's a smart thought, as well, to flicker eyes quickly as they pursue descending trip of the ball. This avoids "dazzle stumbles.") On pop-ups that go toward the rear of the catcher, the turn brought about by the undercut of the bat frequently makes the ball bend as it goes up.

When in doubt, it will bend toward the player if he undermines an outside pitch and far from him if the angle is inside. In this way, if the ball goes up over the catcher's left shoulder, he should swing on his right side to return and under. That way, he will, for the most part, discover the ball bending toward him, making the catch a lot simpler. If the ball goes up over the right shoulder, the catcher should swing left to pursue it.

Catchers Cover third

There are multiple times when the catcher in baseball covers third. The first and most significant is a piece of his task in the hit guard with a sprinter on first. The catcher rushes into the jewel on the hit, however, if the third baseman fields the ball, he circles to his left and hustles to third. If he doesn't do that, the base will be open and the sprinter progressing from first to second can keep on the third.

The catcher additionally every so often winds up on third amid a summary among home and third. He again goes to third when both the shortstop and second baseman pursue a pop fly straightforwardly toward the rear of second with sprinters on base. (Third baseman takes second, pitcher covers home.) It's a smart thought for catchers to back up first when the plates are vacant, and the hitter hits a grounder to the infield. This is particularly significant in a nearby ball game. The catcher, to make this back-up play, should begin running at the split of the bat and head for a spot something like 20 feet to the foul side of first. In this way, if the ball gets by the respectable starting point man, the catcher and ball will touch base at about a similar time and the catcher will most likely either hold the sprinter on first or nip him going into second if he endeavors to progress.

Speeding The Game Of Baseball Up

It might snow where you're found or less - 20 degrees, however in what will appear a squint of the eye; spring preparing will open, joined by the common new beginning sentiments of a fresh start.

Lamentably, the baseball chief and group proprietors will do their depiction of our current "do nothing" Congress, by discussing goals to issues they as of now have the instruments, yet come up short on the guts, to amend.

One such serious issue is the gradualness and period it takes to play a noteworthy association baseball match-up. Each one needs to discuss it. However, nobody needs to fix it.

These wealthy person group proprietors guarantee they are worried about the fans' advantage, yet in all actuality, they are concerned about TV income, yet whatever the inspiration they as of now have the mallet they have to speed the diversion up immediately.

Baseball Rule 8.04(b), regularly known as the 12 following guideline has been available to them for a long while, and although it may not tackle each issue, upholding the standard would take a massive lump of sat idle out of the length of a baseball match-up.

Just characterized, the standard states without any sprinters on base, the pitcher has 12 seconds from getting the ball once again from the catcher, to toss the next pitch to the hitter. That may not appear to be a great deal of time, however, actualize the activity yourself of toeing the elastic, getting your sign and starting your windup, and I'm sure you'll understand it's more than satisfactory.

What am I proposing to do, add another umpire to put a stopwatch on the pitcher? By and by the work has just been accomplished for the proprietors and chief "On the most proficient method to actualize the standard" by baseball's TV World Series foe, the NFL.

Any individual who pursues football knows the 5-yard postponement of diversion punishment when the offense surpasses it's distributed time to get a playoff, along these lines is punished.

Do the arbitrators and the quarterbacks have a stopwatch dangling around their neck to always look at? Not, however, what they do have is a vast tally down the clock, which ticks down the distributed time, situated on the two closures of the arena for the quarterback to effectively observe and know how much time he has to get a playoff or endure a punishment.

Since baseball as of now has the standard, they should merely authorize it, and another person previously gave them the strategy for executing the norm, you'd figure the MLB could, at any rate, make sense of where to find the tally down clock, or two whenever considered necessary, where every single concerned gathering could without much of a stretch view it.

Presently I know real alliance baseball is "Enormous Business" with billions of dollars in income yearly and shouldn't be dealt with like a youth baseball association, however with regards to the competitors' perspective or feelings, don't attempt to persuade mean MLB pitcher has any more weight on him than the multi-year old endeavoring to contribute out of a sketchy situation a title amusement. Weight is weight, and there's no requirement for the adult competitor to require 30 seconds to gather himself when a multi-year old can do it in 8 seconds.

Seven Steps on How to Hit a Baseball

Hitting a baseball is a standout amongst the most challenging activities in games. It requires investment and a ton of training to run one without flaw. There are seven essential strides in hitting a baseball that I have utilized and ought to be accustomed to hitting a baseball appropriately.

Selecting the bat is an essential advance in hitting a baseball. You shouldn't choose a bat that is excessively overwhelming or unreasonably long for yourself. For a beginner the lighter the bat, the better it is to rehearse and learn. As you figure out how to hit a baseball, you can choose a bat that is progressively agreeable for you to utilize. One method for doing this is holding the bat straight out. If you can keep the bat straight out without it twisting the bat, it is ideal for you.

Your stance is an essential piece of your swing. You should have a strong position that is agreeable for you. Stances can fluctuate from various perspectives, upstanding, hunkered, open, and shut stances, are principle regions that stances can be utilized. Pick one and if you are alright with the attitude keep using it. Your position is the batter's container likewise assists with your stance. You can stand anyplace you need inside the container however you don't need an excessively wide of a position since you won't get enough power out of your swing.

The grasp you have on the handle of the bat is the critical second advance to your swing. You ought to have a firm hold on the bat yet not very tight. If you are correct handed, your right hand is on top, and your left hand is on the base, the other way around for lefties. You would prefer not to stifle the handle since that worries your muscles. You ought to have the capacity to move the bat in a roundabout movement in your hands to realize that your hold is excellent.

In the wake of venturing into the batter's crate, you ought to concentrate on the pitcher. Both of your eyes ought to pursue the ball the entire time. If you are following the ball splendidly, you should recognize what kind of pitch it is and where the area will be directly out of the pitcher's hand.

Your walk is the last advance in your swing. The step triggers your entire body. It makes a flood of vitality from your legs as far as possible up to your arms and shoulders. Your level shouldn't be any more extended than a foot. When your foot contacts down your wings are prepared to finish.

The way to hitting a baseball is a dimension swing. Continuously endeavor to keep the barrel of the bat level with the idea of the baseball. Along these lines, you have a less wiggle room. If your bat is level, you can, in any case, get a hit greater part of the time. You can somewhat be beneath or over the ball and still can get a hit.

After associating with the ball, you should finish. Try not to stop when you hit the ball, proceed through the ball. If you terminate your swing, you lose all the power that you have made previously. After you swing your bat ought to have the capacity to contact the back of your shoulder.

The most effective method to Analyze a Baseball Swing

Numerous individuals who have the essential information of baseball can take a gander at an unpracticed hitter and make sense of what they are fouling up. Certain things like venturing out, over-striding, swinging early or late, uppercutting, pulling off the ball and taking their eye off the ball are genuinely obvious imperfections. The answers for these issues are not as self-evident, and not as necessary as just telling the hitter what they are fouling up. Muscle memory can be hard to change, and it is significant for hitters and grown-ups to have persistence with players who are endeavoring to make changes to their muscle memory. In any case, I am losing track of what's most important. The swing can't be fixed until it has been breaking down effectively. Examining a swing when the blemishes are not as clear takes a substantially more experienced mentor.

Following are pointers for mentors who are not as experienced to comprehend what to search for while dissecting a baseball swing:

1. The best point to watch a hitter is the side edge, as from the on-deck circle.

2.The primary concern to watch from this edge is the way of the bat barrel.

3.The perfect is the point at which the bat barrel settles over the hitter's back shoulder with the handle of the bat pointing down similarly as the front foot lands with the walk. A slight tilt of the bat barrel where it settles anyplace somewhere in the range of 11 and 1 o'clock is ideal.

4.From this settled position, the perfect is to see the hands and barrel start on a descending way towards the ball, while never voyaging a long way excessively from the hitters head on the way to the ball. This is known as a reduced swing.

5.The swing is started by a crush of the spirit knee enabling the hips to open, and with a draw of the first hand.

6.The bat barrel begins a descending way yet will start to level off rapidly, particularly on the lower pitches. As the back knee pivots towards the ball, the back elbow brings and stays exceptionally close down to the body on the underlying part of the swing. This keeps the hands from throwing far from the body, another essential imperfection of youthful hitters.

7.This leveling off is cultivated by the hands framing a palm-up (top side) and palm-down (lower side) position when contact. The hands will finish at about a similar dimension; they started the swing, at shoulder level stature.

8.In the wake of leveling off, great hitters will keep the bat for the most part level for an extended period until well after contact when it will start an upward way till completing behind the back.

9.As the bat barrel gets through, the hitter's hips have opened with the paunch catch confronting the pitcher.

10. The zone between the legs should shape a capital An at contact, with the hitters head situated over the back hip.

11. The back foot has turned towards the pitcher as the weight has moved from the hind leg towards the front foot, and the hitter will wrap up on his rear toe.

12. The majority of this is in a perfect world finished with the hitters head and eyes following the ball right till contact.

Regularly, it takes a lot of perception of the baseball swing to get on these little complexities of the swing. These activities of the swing happen all around rapidly. Envisioning a plane arrival is a decent personality representation that portrays the bat barrel swing way. As referenced, giving close consideration to the form of the bat barrel is the way to dissecting the swing. Watching video of good hitters, particularly in moderate movement, can be useful in figuring out how to break down the baseball swing. Big rhythms involve excellent balance, even though there is a touchy opening of the hips and a forceful "toss" of the hands. In the entirety of my long periods of showing hitting, I found that if I could address the hitter's bat way, the remainder of their issues started to vanish or were a lot simpler to solve.

In the wake of viewing a hitter from the side edge, it is advantageous to break down the swing from the edge of the pitcher or straightforwardly behind the hitter. From these edges, it is simpler to see the hitter's front side, principally the walk heading and front shoulder. It is significant that the hitter's walk is towards the pitcher and that their front shoulder remains pointed at the ball until the swing starts; when the front shoulder will begin its pivot open.

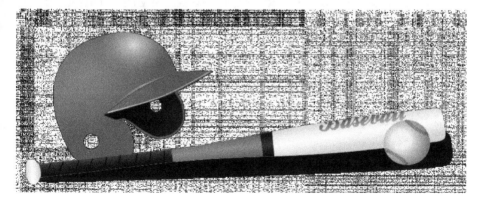

CHAPTER THREE
How to Pitch a Baseball: A Detailed Description of the Sequence of Moves

Pitching may resemble a simple motion of merely tossing a baseball. However, there is very part of abilities engaged with it. These attitudes take a great deal of preparing and practice to get. Here's a manual for the real parts of pitching that you have to ace. While the vast majority of the depictions are gone for right-gave pitchers, you can undoubtedly adjust them to yourself if you are left-given.

We should begin off with pitching from the breeze up, which is most ordinarily rehearsed by youthful players. Position your feet on the elastic about shoulder-width apart. Your toes ought to point towards the home plate. The main pieces of your feet that ought to be on the elastic are your impact points. Your toes ought to be before the elastic. While holding the ball in your gloved hand, broaden your turn before you.

Get a decent hold on the ball. Keep the ball covered up, so your opponents won't realize which pitch you are going to toss. Move your left foot in reverse by a couple of inches, and turn your right foot to such an extent that its right side is directly against the edge of the elastic. Your body would naturally be positioned confronting the third base.

Raise your left leg till your thigh is parallel to the parallel to the ground. If you can't keep up your parity in this position, you likely lifted your leg to an extreme.

Do the accompanying developments at the same time: Move both your gloved and tossing hands separated from one another and downwards, while you bring down your lifted left leg downwards. Your left leg ought to be practically straight when your arms have been brought down.

As your left leg contacts the ground, move your weight to your right leg while somewhat bowing this leg. This will give you extra influence later on when you push off from the elastic. Skim your left foot outwards until it's pointing towards the home plate. As you move the left foot, your right leg should begin pushing off to gather speed. All through these developments, you ought to keep up your chest area's position looking towards the third base. Likewise, while your left foot is floating outwards, your arms ought to have completed their round motion and the two have climbed into the tossing position.

Your left foot ought to keep up a shut point when it lands. Your toes ought not to be pointing towards home plate as of now. When your left leg hits the ground, your right leg will feel the force and would be raised very high. Exploit the energy by turning your hips around to produce more power from your center. This is the moment that you discharge the ball.

Having discharged the ball, you have to pursue the mechanics of wrapping up. This is significant in anticipating wounds to your arm. Give your arm a chance to proceed in its descending swing, in the meantime as the finish of your back leg. Your end position ought to be with a practically straight back and with your feet evenly positioned to one another.

Distinctive Types of Pitches in Baseball

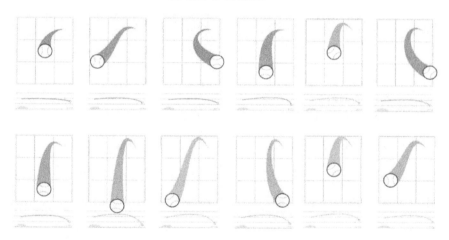

Pitches are isolated into three as fastballs, breaking balls and changeups. Fastballs can be tossed quick. It is the most widely recognized pitch and can be tossed around 90 miles for each hour. Fastballs are hurled at velocities of 95- 104 mph and up to 107.9 mph. Fastballs are separated into different kinds like four crease fastball, two crease fastball, shaper, forkball, and splitter. In four crease fastball grasp the ball with your record and center finger together over the horseshoe crease with your fingers spread separated marginally. Ensure your fingertips are a tad over the bands. It is ordinarily the quickest pitch a player has and can get as high as 100+mph. This fastball doesn't have much development, as pitchers attempt and toss it past you. Two-crease fastball is otherwise called sinker.

The two-crease fastball has all the more descending development amid pitch. Shaper is a mix of slider and fastball. A forkball has a forward turn. The contrast among splitter and forkball is that the spacer has a steep drop to it and the forkball has to a greater extent a continuous decline. A pitcher who utilizes principally breaking ball pitches is frequently alluded to as a junkballer. A breaking ball is more troublesome than a fastball for a catcher to get as they here and there hit the ground before making it to the plate. Breaking balls are isolated into three as a curveball, slider, and screwball. In curveball, a pitcher puts a top to turn on a contribute request for the ball to break or bend. A slider has more speed than a curveball, yet less rate than a fastball. The screwball breaks the other way.

Changeups are isolated into palm ball, circle change, super changeup. Practice the palm ball by utilizing more tightly, and looser grasps until you discover how you can toss the pitch all the more adequately. In baseball, circle changeup is a pitch thrown with a hold that incorporates circle data, thus the name. The super changeup is essentially a changeup that has a more significant speed respectful among it and the fastball. Different sorts of pitches incorporate knuckleball, Eephus Pitch, spitball and gyro ball. The knuckleball is tossed for having as meager turn on the ball as could be allowed. The Eephus pitch is a contribution that is thrown a high curve. A spitball is a pitch that will have spit or some other sort of fluid on it. A Gyro ball is a pitch that will have a bullet like a turn.

Baseball Drills - Infield Crispness is Key

A crisp infield amid a diversion is moving and rousing for all on the team. It's additionally unsatisfying for the other side when they don't coordinate a similar dimension of snap, zip, and crispness. A group of infielders who gangs this aptitude created through purposeful baseball drills will set the beat of a diversion. On the other side, a sluggish and messy infield won't make certainty for the remainder of the team and ought to be kept away from at all costs.

Here are two different ways to build up the exceptionally significant crispness factor for infielders.

1.Physical crispness is shown first by hustle on and off the field. A team, and particularly an infield, that is very purposeful about how they take to the field demands regard. It demonstrates center, enthusiasm, and above all else a simple way to deal with kicking the others teams' butt. Be that as it may, this expertise must be educated from the very first moment of exercises. A mentor that gives little consideration to this detail and after that endeavor to set up it mid-season will battle to do as such. Amid baseball penetrates by and by infielders should hard to positions, and if the objective isn't accomplished, everybody returns on to the hole and attempts once more. The image gets crosswise over rapidly. The uplifting news is, not many teams do this; along these lines, a decent organization will emerge right away.

2.Another presentation of physical hustle comes through tossing the ball around the infield after a strikeout. If your team is in the propensity for throwing the ball around the diamond (and they ought to be) after a restricting hitter strikes out, be smart about it. Infielders ought to decrease the separation from one another by a decent five stages. Developments ought to imitate the kind of briskness one would show in playing out a double play. I can't accentuate enough the significance of making this part perfect and free of mistake in no way like a quick and exact toss around after a strikeout to keep protective spirits high.

3. The last abilities take more time and center to ace. It requires more mental concentrate as opposed to past two which required physical concentration and planning. A team that speaks with the pitcher and each other resembles an ensemble loaded up with an agreement. Baseball shouldn't be played quietly, yet then again, shouldn't be played with outlandish hints of "hello player hitter, swing!" This isn't correspondence, yet rather (to keep with the music subject of this passage) sounds like a battling youthful musician irritating his folks in the family room! Infielders ought to help the pitcher to remember where he should be on hit resistance when there are runners on base for potential pickoffs, and so forth. Infielders ought to speak with one another on situating with runners on base, shorts, and so on. Like I said before, this must be polished reliably amid all baseball drills. Correspondence must be an original piece of the play of the team, and not constrained.

Baseball Coaching Digest - Baseball Rules - Understanding the "Infield Fly" Rule

The "In-field Fly" rule is a standout amongst the scariest, confounding, and misjudged controls in baseball. The standard is regularly a point of discussion among coaches, players, and observers watching the diversion. Many ask, "For what reason do we have the 'In-field" fly standard? When does the "In-field Fly" baseball rule apply? Here I diagram the explanation behind this standard of baseball, the circumstances under which this baseball rule applies, and other data to enable you to all the more likely have a superior comprehension of it.

For what reason do we have the "In-field" fly guideline?

The expressed reason for the infield fly guideline, in most baseball rule books, is that the standard is implemented to keep a guarded player from dropping a fly ball intentionally or giving an infield a chance to fly drop to the ground immaculate to endeavor to turn a double play.

For instance, there are runners at first, and a respectable halfway point without any outs. The third shortstop is handling a high pop fly hit high among him and a modest halfway point. When we didn't have the "In-Field-Fly" rule, he could give it a chance to drop. Lift it up and rapidly contact a respectable halfway point, at that point toss to third to get a tag on a decent halfway point runner for the double play. The barrier has turned a simple twofold game. The two runners being compelled to tag up on the set get no opportunity of progressing to the following base to forestall the outs.

Another situation would be bases stacked, and an infield fly is hit high that will arrive three feet before home plate. The catcher sets up to make the catch. He enables the ball to hit. He rapidly lifts it, contacts home plate for the first out and after that, he tosses the ball to the third baseman who is set up on the sack. The third baseman catches the ball, labels the base for the second out, and after that tosses to a respectable halfway point for the finished triple play. If there was no infield fly principle, the accompanying could occur: Runners are on first and second with under two outs. A pop fly is hit to the third baseman. He deliberately drops the fly ball, lifts it, labels third and after that makes the toss to a respectable halfway point to finish a double play. It is a pure triple play since every one of the three runners is labeling up on their bases in the expectation that the ball to be gotten.

What are the circumstances in which the standard applies?

The standard is appropriate with a runner at first and second, or first, second and third bases with under two outs.

6 Essential Things to Remember about the Infield-Fly Rule:

1.The standard is connected on any reasonable fly ball that could have been gotten by an infielder with customary exertion. The ball does not need to be understood. The hitter is pronounced out quickly when the ball is hit. The out stands if the ball an is in a reasonable area.

2.The ball does not need to be in the infield. It tends to be in the outfield. The key is if an infielder, as indicated by the judgment of the umpire, ought to have the capacity to get the fly ball with moderate exertion.

3.If the umpires summon the standard and an outfielder catches the ball, the out still stand. If the ball land an uncaught in a reasonable area, the out still stands.

4.When the umpire has called the standard. The other base runners may progress at their very own hazard. When they endeavor to advance and are labeled out, the outcome is a second out on the play. The runners can improve after labeling up like they would on a fly ball. The distinction for the runner is that since the hitter is out, there is never again a power play and the runner does not have to progress, regardless of whether the ball isn't gotten.

5.An infield fly principle must be considered when the ball is noticeable all around. The flag given by the umpires is blamed dealing into the air.

6.The fly ball must be in a reasonable area. The umpires will make a verbal call, "Hitter is out if the ball is reasonable."

A Peek on the Major League Baseball Records

Baseball has been an amusement that numerous individuals are keen on. There are now innumerable players that make it to the top and have indicated incredible scores for the groups that they are playing for time given. There are first league baseball records that are consistently refreshed as more players that perform well keep on appearing changed type of playing.

Realizing these players will give anybody a superior comprehension of the diversion and valuing their capacities can put anybody at wonder. The Major League baseball records show distinctive competitors that have contributed significantly to the historical backdrop of baseball.

There are a few records that are out limited by more current files, yet there are some that have kept on standing to confirm after some time. These untouched most loved records done by incredible competitors are increasing greater prominence over baseball aficionados.

There are books, online articles, and sites that handle distinctive records. Understanding and valuing these records would be a significant factor for a baseball buff. Consistently, there is a record on which player did a difficult job and made through it. As the year's pass, another player outstands the past, and the rundown is consistently refreshed. Additional books are looking at the step by step players.

The Major League baseball records may be a rundown of best players amid their time yet it can influence a player to comprehend the diversion in a more profound point of view. The pioneers of the league for a given time implied an excellent deal for the players amid their time. So having a look at them today will give anybody a more clear view on how the amusement continued amid their time.

Baseball Coaching - How To Coach Baseball For Players 12 and Under

There is a whole other world to baseball training than just procedure and fundamentals. While these are significant, I am going to cover the viewpoints that I feel will enable you to turn into the best mentor you can be.

Baseball Coaching Tip #1 - Patience

Without persistence, you're in for a long season. Particularly at this youthful age with aptitude levels being so uncommon from player to player and hormones just beginning to kick in (clearly relying upon age), you should practice outrageous persistence. Everything from the persistence of a child not having the capacity to complete a drill accurately to a child misbehaving. You, as a rule, don't have the foggiest idea of what is happening at their home. It's terrible; they are in; baseball training might be their break, regardless of whether they don't act like it at times. Keep in mind, and no one said this was simple, and you positively aren't managing robots so make sure to be persistent consistently...

Baseball Coaching Tip #2 - Self-Control

Now and again you will need to tear your hair out and might be so disappointed with a player, not really how he is performing, yet how is he acting that you'll need to thro impulse off the group. Presently this isn't politically right. However, you'd kid yourself if you figured this didn't occur in each adolescent league the nation over. It's at these occasions where you'll be a pioneer to these young men, which leads into my next tip...

Baseball Coaching Tip #3 - Leadership

These young men admire you. How you act will help shape them now and later on. Incredible baseball instructing is done continuously in a positive design. There will never be an opportunity to be negative, particularly at this youthful age. Show others how it is done and be positive and supporting.

Baseball Coaching Tip #4 - Instill Self-Esteem

The more significant part of the messes with you will won't be extraordinary competitors or baseball players. You'll be fortunate to have 1 or 2 players who will even play in secondary school, let alone in the Major Leagues. The confidence they gain from you will help them in each part of their life. Be positive, strengthen positives again and again. This does not mean they shouldn't be adequately trained and educated, don't concentrate on anything negative.

Baseball Coaching Tip #5 - Fundamentals

In many records, you would have discovered this at #1. Truth is it's merely not significant on the grand plan of things as 1-4 on this rundown. Try not to misunderstand me, and you ought to do your best to show your children the proper fundamentals of the amusement: hitting, tossing, getting and running. Try not to stress over cutting edge systems or any of that nonsense. That stuff will descend the line if they are as yet playing in secondary school or school. Concentrate on what will get them there, which is proper baseball fundamentals.

Baseball Coaching Tip #6 - Mental Aspect Of Baseball

This is significant in baseball instructing because much the same as Yogi said: "90 of the diversion is half mental". As it were - it's essential to progress, in baseball as well as life. Incredible hitters fall flat 70% of the time. Incredible agents and ladies come up short at a much higher rate, yet they get back up and continue attempting. Managing disappointment is the mystery in baseball and life that everybody's searching for. Be positive, provide some guidance to gain from errors and push ahead.

Baseball Coaching Tip # 7 - Ability To Deal With Parents

This is a big deal, for the most part, to make your life simpler toward the start of the period set standard procedures for the guardians. Things, for example, no shouting, not conversing with children amid the diversion, not hindering at training, and so on. Whatever you feel good with. Set these guidelines early, both verbally and on paper and it will be evident to all if any standards are broken.

Coaching Youth Baseball - Tips to Be Successful Without Alienating Parents

Each parent needs their kid to be fruitful in sports. Youth baseball is regularly the dominant sport in which a tyke takes part. Baseball is "America's Game." Youth baseball shows one of a kind tests to those that mentor. Notwithstanding the undertaking of teaching youthful youngsters, the sport and its numerous features, the mentor of a young baseball team should likewise communicate with the guardians of the kids on the side.

Kids are acquainted with this team sport as right on time as five years old. Guardians regularly become coaches as of now because they feel their tyke will show signs of improvement chance to play. Each parent, regardless of whether a mentor or not, need their kid to be the team's headliner. This will without doubt cause conflicts between coaches and guardians.

Tips to be Successful Without Alienating Parents

1. The reason for the mentor in youth baseball is to show kids how to play the sport of baseball and to cooperate in a team setting.

2.You ought to have careful learning and comprehension of the guidelines of youth baseball and the group in which you are training.

3.Treat each tyke on your team reasonably and give each an equal chance to play each position.

4.Try not to indicate a bias to any of the players on your team, particularly your youngster.

5.Comprehend that triumphant isn't all that matters. It is increasingly significant that the kids take part and have a great time as opposed to stressing over the ultimate result of an amusement.

6.Continuously keep up your attention on showing the basics of the amusement.

7.Plan your practices and the basics you expect to instruct at each ahead of time and adhere to your agenda.

8.Make your practices instructive and fun. You will keep your players consideration and help them learn and hold the exercises being educated.

9.Impart a feeling of order and pride in your players. Instruct them to tune in, adhere to directions and invest wholeheartedly in their achievements both on and off the field.

10.Offer consolation and backing to your players when botches are made. Downplay analysis.

Following these tips will enable you to be fruitful as a young baseball mentor and will avoid estranging the guardians of your team individuals. Your prosperity as a mentor ought to be estimated by the information and valuation for the amusement you impart in your players, not by the number of recreations won. Keep in mind that consider it. With just extreme individual cases, significant league baseball pitchers, probably the best competitors on the planet, are utterly awful at batting. You would imagine that they would be a portion of the absolute best hitters since they as far as anyone knows can envision the pitcher superior to most different players. What's more, those of us who played little league baseball unquestionably recollect those folks who were incredible pitchers just as extraordinary hitters- - truth be told, that appeared to go connected at the hip a lot of the time. In any case, that is not the situation in the significant leagues. Dominant league pitching itself is such requesting craftsmanship that pitchers need to invest the more substantial part of their training energy pitching- - not taking batting practice.

Along these lines, even though they may have a ton of natural ability, not many of them can also be equipped with significant leagues, baseball hitters. Their baseball preparing naturally doesn't fall into that class.

If you see, you'll see that most catchers aren't anything superior to fair hitters, either, although they surely are superior to pitchers and there are some of them who are genuine batting champions. The baseball preparing of catchers, as well, is all the more particular.

12 Steps for Parent and Coach Relationship

STEP ONE

When defined the right way, competition in youth sports is both good and healthy and teaches children a variety of important life skills. The word "compete" comes from the Latin words "com" and "petere" which mean together and seeking respectively. The true definition of competition is a seeking together where your opponent is your partner, not the enemy! The better he performs, the more chance you have of having a peak performance. Sports is about learning to deal with challenges and obstacles. Without a worthy opponent, without any challenges sports is not so much fun. The more the challenge the better the opportunity you have to go beyond your limits.

STEP TWO

ENCOURAGE YOUR CHILD TO COMPETE AGAINST HIMSELF The ultimate goal of the sport experience is to challenge oneself and continually improve. Unfortunately, judging improvement by winning and losing is both an unfair and inaccurate measure.

Winning in sports is about doing the best you can do, separate from the outcome or the play of your opponent. Children should be encouraged to compete against their own potential (i.e., Peter and Patty Potential). That is, the boys should focus on beating "Peter", competing against themselves, while the girls challenge "Patty". When your child has this focus and plays to better himself instead of beating someone else, he will be more relaxed, have more fun and therefore perform better

STEP THREE

DO NOT DEFINE SUCCESS AND FAILURE IN TERMS OF WINNING AND LOSING A corollary to TWO, one of the main purposes of the youth sports experience is skill acquisition and mastery. When a child performs to his potential and loses it is criminal to focus on the outcome and become critical. If a child plays his very best and loses, you need to help him feel like a winner! Similarly, when a child or team performs far below their potential but wins, this is not cause to feel like a winner. Help your child make this important separation between success and failure and winning and losing. Remember, if you define success and failure in terms of winning and losing, you're playing a losing game with your child!

STEP FOUR

BE SUPPORTIVE, DO NOT COACH! Your role on the parent-coach-athlete team is as a Support player with a capital S! You need to be your child's best fan. unconditionally! Leave the coaching and instruction to the coach. Provide encouragement, support, empathy, transportation, money, help with fund-raisers, etc., but... do not coach! Most parents that get into trouble with their children do so because they forget to remember the important position that they play.

Coaching interferes with your role as supporter and fan. The last thing your child needs and wants to hear from you after a disappointing performance or loss is what they did technically or strategically wrong. Keep your role as a parent on the team separate from that as coach, and, if by necessity you actually get stuck in the almost no-win position of having to coach your child, try to maintain this separation of roles (i.e. on the deck, field or court say, "Now I'm talking to you as a coach", at home say, "Now I'm talking to you as a parent"). Don't parent when you coach and don't coach at home when you're supposed to be parenting.

STEP FIVE

HELP MAKE THE SPORT FUN FOR YOUR CHILD It's a time proven principle of peak performance that the more fun an athlete is having, the more they will learn and the better they will perform. Fun must be present for peak performance to happen at every level of sports from youth to world class competitor! When a child stops having fun and begins to dread practice or competition, it's time for you as a parent to become concerned! When the sport or game becomes too serious, athletes have a tendency to burn out and become susceptible to repetitive performance problems.

An easy rule of thumb: If your child is not enjoying what they are doing, nor loving the heck out of it, investigate! What is going on that's preventing them from having fun? Is it the coaching? The pressure? Is it you?! Keep in mind that being in a highly competitive program does not mean that there is no room for fun. The child that continues to play long after the fun is going will soon become a drop out statistic.

STEP SIX

WHOSE GOAL IS IT? FIVE leads us to a very important question! Why is your child participating in the sport? Are they doing it because they want to, for them, or because of you. When they have problems in their sport do you talk about them as "our" problems, "our jump isn't high enough", "we're having trouble with our flip turn" , etc. Are they playing because they don't want to disappoint you, because they know how important the sport is to you?

Are they playing for rewards and "bonuses" that you give out? Are their goals and aspirations yours or theirs? How invested are you in their success and failure? If they are competing to please you or for your vicarious glory they are in it for the wrong reasons! Further, if they stay involved for you, ultimately everyone will lose. It is quite normal and healthy to want your child to excel and be as successful as possible. But, you cannot make this happen by pressuring them with your expectations or by using guilt or bribery to keep them involved. If they have their own reasons and own goals for participating, they will be far more motivated to excel and therefore far more successful.

STEP SEVEN

YOUR CHILD IS NOT HIS PERFORMANCE-LOVE HIM UNCONDITIONALLY Do not equate your child's self-worth and lovability with his performance. The most tragic and damaging mistake I see parents continually make is punishing a child for a bad performance by withdrawing emotionally from him. A child loses a race, strikes out or misses and easy shot on goal and the parent responds with disgust, anger and withdrawal of love and approval. CAUTION: Only use this strategy if you want to damage your child emotionally and ruin your relationship with him. In the 1988 Olympics, when Greg Louganis needed and got a perfect 10 on his last dive to overtake the Chinese diver for the gold medal, his last thought before he went was, "If I don't make it, my mother will still love me".

STEP EIGHT

REMEMBER THE IMPORTANCE OF SELF-ESTEEM IN ALL OF YOUR INTERACTIONS WITH YOUR CHILD-ATHLETE
Athletes of all ages and levels perform in direct relationship to how they feel about themselves. When your child is in an athletic environment that boosts his self-esteem, he will learn faster, enjoy himself more and perform better under competitive pressure. One thing we all want as children and never stop wanting is to be loved and accepted, and to have our parents feel good about what we do. This is how self-esteem gets established. When your interactions with your child make him feel good about himself, he will, in turn, learn to treat himself this very same way.

This does not mean that you have to incongruently compliment your child for a great effort after they have just performed miserably. In this situation being empathic and sensitive to his feelings is what's called for. Self esteem makes the world go round. Make your child feel good about himself and you've given him a gift that lasts a lifetime. Do not interact with your child in a way that assaults his self-esteem by degrading, embarrassing or humiliating him. If you continually put your child down or minimize his accomplishments not only will he learn to do this to himself throughout his life, but he will also repeat your mistake with his children!

STEP NINE

GIVE YOUR CHILD THE GIFT OF FAILURE If you really want your child to be as happy and as successful as possible in everything that he does, teach him how to fail! The most successful people in and out of sports do two things differently than everyone else. First,, they are more willing to take risks and therefore fail more frequently. Second, they use their failures in a positive way as a source of motivation and feedback to improve. Our society is generally negative and teaches us that failure is bad, a cause for humiliation and embarrassment, and something to be avoided at all costs.

Fear of failure or humiliation causes one to be tentative and non-active. In fact, most performance blocks and poor performances are a direct result of the athlete being preoccupied with failing or messing up. You can't learn to walk without falling enough times. Each time that you fall your body gets valuable information on how to do it better. You can't be successful or have peak performances if you are concerned with losing or failing. Teach your child how to view setbacks, mistakes and risk-taking positively and you'll have given him the key to a lifetime of success. Failure is the perfect stepping stone to success.

STEP TEN

CHALLENGE, DON'T THREATEN Many parents directly or indirectly use guilt and threats as a way to "motivate" their child to perform better. Performance studies clearly indicate that while threats may provide short term results, the long term costs in terms of psychological health and performance are devastating. Using fear as a motivator is probably one of the worst dynamics you could set up with your child.

Threats take the fun out of performance and directly lead to your child performing terribly. implicit in a threat, (do this or else!) is your own anxiety that you do not believe the child is capable. Communicating this lack of belief, even indirectly is further devastating to the child's performance. A challenge does not entail loss or negative consequences should the athlete fail. Further, implicit in a challenge is the empowering belief, "I think that you can do it".

STEP ELEVEN

STRESS PROCESS, NOT OUTCOME When athletes choke under pressure and perform far below their potential, a very common cause of this is a focus on the outcome of the performance (i.e., win/lose, instead of the process). In any peak performance, the athlete is totally oblivious to the outcome and instead is completely absorbed in the here and now of the actual performance.

An outcome focus will almost always distract and tighten up the athlete insuring a bad performance. Furthermore focusing on the outcome, which is completely out of the athlete's control will raise his anxiety to a performance inhibiting level. So if you truly want your child to win, help get his focus away from how important the contest is and have them focus on the task at hand. Supportive parents de-emphasize winning and instead stress learning the skills and playing the game.

STEP TWELVE

AVOID COMPARISONS AND RESPECT DEVELOPMENTAL DIFFERENCES

Supportive parents do not use other athletes that their child competes against to compare and thus evaluate their child's progress. Comparisons are useless, inaccurate and destructive. Each child matures differently and the process of comparison ignores significant distorting effects of developmental differences.

For example, two 12 year old boys may only have their age in common! One may physically have the build and perform like a 16 year old while the other, a late developer, may have the physical size and attribute of a 9 year old. Performance comparisons can prematurely turn off otherwise talented athletes on their sport. The only value of comparisons is in teaching. If one child demonstrates proper technique, that child can be used comparatively as a model only! For your child to do his very best he needs to learn to stay within himself. Worrying about how another athlete is doing interferes with him doing this.

your job as a mentor is to teach, advance enthusiasm for the sport and, most importantly, to have some good times. In doing as such, you will find that conflicts with your players' folks will be kept to a base and make an increasingly pleasant encounter for everybody included.

CONCLUSION

Numerous individuals appear to trust that baseball hitting at an elite dimension is only some typical athletic capacity that a few people have while the vast majority don't. Excellent baseball hitting requires great baseball preparing in the science and craft of batting.

The facts demonstrate that some current capacities are required with the end goal for one to can turn into an excellent hitter in baseball. For example, a .400 hitter will never be except if he has a shared vision, with the goal that he's ready to get the ball from the soonest point in the pitcher's conveyance and afterward read the turning of the creases in incredible detail. Also, honestly, there needs to be a special present for essential dexterity.

Hitting a baseball well is broadly viewed as the absolute most troublesome accomplishment in all of pro athletics, everything considered. The baseball hitter needs to utilize a round stick to hit a round ball, and that ball is moving quickly (some of the time VERY quickly) over a short separation and has been tossed by somebody who is proposing to make that ball miss the bat. Also, that is all pretty much reaching the ball. At that point, there's where the contact should be adequate that it gives the hitter's group some offense!

In this way, genuinely, there's something else entirely to batting than meets the eye with regards to baseball hitting. Brain and body need to work as one to accomplish successful hitting results. What's more, that is just not going to happen except if there is some excellent baseball preparing in hitting.

Consider it. With just extreme individual cases, significant league baseball pitchers, probably the best competitors on the planet, are utterly awful at batting. You would imagine that they would be a portion of the absolute best hitters since they as far as anyone knows can envision the pitcher superior to most different players. What's more, those of us who played little league baseball unquestionably recollect those folks who were incredible pitchers just as extraordinary hitters- - truth be told, that appeared to go connected at the hip a lot of the time. In any case, that is not the situation in the significant leagues. Dominant league pitching itself is such requesting craftsmanship that pitchers need to invest the more substantial part of their training energy pitching- - not taking batting practice.

Along these lines, even though they may have a ton of natural ability, not many of them can also be equipped with significant leagues, baseball hitters. Their baseball preparing naturally doesn't fall into that class.

If you see, you'll see that most catchers aren't anything superior to fair hitters, either, although they surely are superior to pitchers and there are some of them who are genuine batting champions. The baseball preparing of catchers, as well, is all the more very particular to concentrate on the incredibly hard to an ace arrangement of abilities required for getting.

In this way, excellent baseball hitting is painful to the point that the absolute best competitors aren't generally amazing at it- - just because they don't get enough of the particular baseball preparing that makes great hitters.

Something else to consider is that excellent baseball hitting is so hard to ace that we give Most Valuable Player grants to hitters who get put out 650, 675, 700 times out of each 1,000 at-bats! What's more, if a person makes an out significantly over multiple times for every 1,000 endeavors, yet he can hit that ball a long distance 35 or 40 or numerous times when he DOES reach, we may give him an MVP trophy, as well!

Disclaimer Statement

All information and content contained in this book are provided solely for general information and reference purposes. SSP LLC Limited makes no statement, representation, warranty or guarantee as to the accuracy, reliability or timeliness of the information and content contained in this Book.

Neither SSP Limited or the author of this book nor any of its related company accepts any responsibility or liability for any direct or indirect loss or damage (whether in tort, contract or otherwise) which may be suffered or occasioned by any person howsoever arising due to any inaccuracy, omission, misrepresentation or error in respect of any information and content provided by this book (including any third-party books.

Workout Notes

Workout Notes

Workout Notes

Workout Notes

Workout Notes

Workout Notes

Workout Notes

Workout Notes

Workout Notes

Workout Notes

S.S. Publishing

Printed in the USA
CPSIA information can be obtained
at www.ICGtesting.com
LVHW050503310724
786908LV00001B/60